A study
guide for
Watchman
Nee's

The
Normal
Christian
Life

A study guide for

Watchman Nee's

The Normal Christian Life

by

HARRY FOSTER

CLC ❖ PUBLICATIONS
Fort Washington, Pennsylvania 19034

Published by CLC Publications

U.S.A.
P.O. Box 1449, Fort Washington, PA 19034

GREAT BRITAIN
51 The Dean, Alresford, Hants. SO24 9BJ

AUSTRALIA
P.O. Box 419M, Manunda, QLD 4879

NEW ZEALAND
10 MacArthur Street, Feilding

ISBN 0-87508-418-4

Copyright © 1976
Harry Foster

First edition 1976
First American edition 1983

This printing 2003

Printed in the United States of America

CONTENTS

NOTE TO OUR READERS

Where reference is made to page numbers in *The Normal Christian Life*, these refer to the American edition of 1977 (and all subsequent reprints). If other editions are used for study, the page numbers may not be the same.

INTRODUCTION

The Normal Christian Life has become a Christian classic with world-wide sales, not only in the original English but also in its many translations.[1]

The Editor's Preface to the third edition points to some of the book's unusual features. One is that this light on God's Word came to us from the Far East, through a comparatively young Chinese who had spent the early years of his life in evangelism and the establishing of Christian churches in his own land. It thus provides striking evidence of how spiritual life and ministry transcends racial and national frontiers.

Then there is the disclosure that Watchman Nee did not prepare this book, and did not even know that it existed. The title is his, and it is composed from spoken messages which he gave while here on a visit to the West. I knew Nee personally and listened to these messages. It is therefore a great joy and a privilege to offer some assistance to readers who propose to study it.

May I reinforce Angus Kinnear's assurance that

[1]Translations have been published in more than twenty languages.

this was never intended as a systematic treatise of Christian doctrine. Nee's only interest was the enlightenment and spiritual growth of God's people. He spoke from his heart to ours. Please keep this fact in mind as you study its chapters. Nothing would have grieved God's servant more than to discover Christians basing their outlook and procedure on "Watchman Nee's teaching." Yet this kind of thing happens, the more so if a teacher has been greatly blessed in his labors, as this one certainly has. Let there be no division, then, based on what the author holds, but let the question always be: "What does the Bible say?" I feel confident that Nee would infinitely prefer to know of God's people who disagreed with him (if that were necessary) and yet were growing in Christ-likeness than to have loyal partisans who used his name and teaching as their court of appeal and yet remained carnal.

Of Watchman Nee's long years of seclusion in a Communist prison we know nothing for certain. We only know that soon after his release in 1972 he went to be with Christ "which is far better." When he was among us, however, we saw in him no merely theoretical expositor but a pattern of humble Christian living. "He was a good man, and full of the Holy Ghost and of faith." Some account of his life and work has been given us in Angus

Kinnear's biography *Against the Tide*.[2]

May I briefly explain this Study Guide. I have done my best to draw attention to salient factors in each chapter by means of some preliminary comments. Then after listing the chapter's sub-headings, I have added ten questions designed to provoke thought and possible discussion. If these are used in a study group, then the leader should not form a mental image of the correct answer in every case with the aim of leading the rest into concurrence with him. Rather he should act as coordinator and reviewer, expecting light to come through from God as the various topics are commented on or even questioned. I say "questioned" because in some cases Nee's ideas may be doubtful or imperfect. The important thing is to avoid contention, wrong dogmatism and unreality, and to maintain hearts and minds always open to the instruction and guidance of the Holy Spirit of God.

[2]Angus I. Kinnear, *Against the Tide*, Christian Literature Crusade, 1973.

CHAPTER ONE

THE BLOOD OF CHRIST

We need to consult the Editor's Note (p. 31) to ensure that we do not make *the blood* a technical term, implying something other or less than the death of Christ on the Cross. In this chapter Nee uses Scripture to emphasize one particular aspect of the redemptive work of the Saviour, employing the term *the blood* to explain the means by which the believer in Christ is delivered from guilt. True to his governing motive, Nee concentrates on the practical effects which result from a clear under-standing of how the Lord's death provides for cleansing and forgiveness. Christian living is not produced by correct theories, nor by the right use of certain phrases, but by fellowship with God. To know in daily experience the constant and lasting effects of the shed blood of Jesus is to become a released personality, enjoying God, helping others, and overcoming evil.

THE BLOOD OF CHRIST

BIBLE READINGS: Romans 3:19-26; Romans 5:1-11

CHAPTER SUB-HEADINGS

QUESTIONS ON CHAPTER ONE

2

THE CROSS OF CHRIST

As we read this chapter we may wish to intrude with theoretical questions or problems based on our personal experiences. We must limit these desires and concentrate on the actual statements before us. Nee affirms that our wrong thoughts and deeds are but the expressions of a wrong or sinful nature.

This confronts us with a dilemma which faced God as well as man, namely: "How can corrupt human nature ever be changed?" The answer is, of course, that it cannot. It must be condemned and rejected; it must be crucified and buried. So Nee points out that Christ's death on the Cross was substitutionary in the fullest sense, i.e., it was an inclusive death. God solved His problem—and ours—by having us crucified.

Presently we shall be allowed to ask questions about the practical outworking of these great truths. How does the Cross really deliver us from the power of a sinful nature passed on through the race? How can we get the benefits of being "in

4

Christ"? That must be left to the next chapters. This study calls for thoughtful and believing acceptance of the Scriptural truths which are set out here. Before we inquire about the experiential aspect, we need to allow the Spirit and the Word to convince us of what the Cross has provided.

THE CROSS OF CHRIST

BIBLE READINGS: Romans 5:12-21; Romans 6:1-6

CHAPTER SUB-HEADINGS

QUESTIONS ON CHAPTER TWO

CHAPTER THREE

THE PATH OF PROGRESS: KNOWING

There are five chapters under the general heading of *The Path of Progress*. They are three, four, six, ten and thirteen. *Knowing* comes first.

This chapter is largely devoted to a re-affirmation of the statements which occupied Chapter Two. We are reminded that we must understand the inclusive nature of Christ's death if we are to experience its power. Nee stresses the historical character of the crucifixion. Whatever my experience may or may not be, I must accept God's stated fact, namely, that it was I who was crucified when the Lord Jesus died on the Cross. The same Bible which tells us that Christ died for us insists that we were together with Him in that crucifixion. Nee calls this "The Gospel for Christians" and reminds us that if we truly believe this we will be spared the frustrating exercise of trying to dominate our old man by the self-effort of repression.

The same faith approach is advocated for sanctification as for justification. Some may feel that

Nee's statements are too sweeping for them and argue that this is an over-simplification of the profound subject of holy living. We must wait to see what he has to say in subsequent chapters.

KNOWING

BIBLE READINGS: Romans 6:1-11; Galatians 2:20

CHAPTER SUB-HEADINGS

QUESTIONS ON CHAPTER THREE

8. "Much of our praying for ourselves is just because we are blind to what God has done." If this is so, to what should most of our praying be directed?   p. 58

9. This chapter stresses "divine revelation." How do you reconcile this with the importance of Scriptural doctrine?   p. 59

10. In what way do you think that Nee's illustration concerning drink factories may fail to present the whole picture of the Christian experience?   p. 60

CHAPTER FOUR

THE PATH OF PROGRESS: RECKONING

As Watchman Nee points out, reckoning or accounting is the one thing which men can do with precision; yet this chapter will probably present us with intellectual problems, and may even leave us feeling rather perplexed mentally.

Now that we reach this call to "reckon," we can see the importance of Chapters Two and Three, for knowing must precede reckoning. Confusion can result from our attempts to obtain deliverance by struggling to make ourselves believe what we know to be unsubstantiated by experience. Nee's remarks here are very much to the point.

The chapter gives us no encouragement to profess or expect sinlessness; it simply reiterates that the way of deliverance is by remembering and relying on the fact that God has included us in Christ's death and resurrection.

Nee insists that the real secret is vital association with the Person of Christ. We must refuse to listen to Satan's misrepresentations. We must learn to reckon on Christ.

12

BIBLE READING: Romans 6:6-14

CHAPTER SUB-HEADINGS

QUESTIONS ON CHAPTER FOUR

CHAPTER FIVE

THE DIVIDE OF THE CROSS

This chapter is parenthetical. It arose from a message which Watchman Nee gave on an occasion of believer's baptism in London. There is fuel for controversy here, both concerning baptism and the parable of grafting. Our wisdom will be to avoid getting caught up with externals so that we can pay attention to the spiritual truth under consideration, namely, the total newness of resurrection life. In Noah's case, of course, the new world was not a sinless one, nor was Noah himself a new man; but the spiritual lessons of the Flood are made very clear, and the baptismal water is seen to be not a symbol of cleansing but of judgment and burial.

Notice Nee's helpful interpretation of Romans 6:2: "You should never have been baptized if you meant to live on in the old realm" (p. 94). This accentuates his point that God does not provide for a mixture of the old with the new but demands that we accept the implications of an entirely **new** life in Christ: the resurrection life which follows crucifixion and burial.

It might be thought that, provided we are prepared to accept our union with Christ in His death, then the experience of resurrection life will follow automatically. This is not the whole truth, though, and perhaps the analogy of grafting brings into view the need for faith's co-operation with God's provision in Christ.

THE DIVIDE OF THE CROSS

BIBLE READINGS: Romans 6:1-4; Galatians 6:14;
1 Peter 3:18-22

CHAPTER SUB-HEADINGS

QUESTIONS ON CHAPTER FIVE

1. Can the old world kingdom be changed into the new kingdom of God? p. 87
2. Name some of the "new faculties" attributed to the new-creation man. p. 88
3. What meaning does Nee give to the word "salvation"? p. 90
4. In the universal "baptism" of Noah's Flood, what was drowned? p. 90
5. Suggest some differences between John's baptism and being baptized into Christ Jesus.
6. Have you any experience of the "tremendous issues" which are provoked by baptism? p. 91
7. Can you find Scriptural justification for Nee's assertion that unless our eyes have been opened to understand death and burial with Christ we have no right

CHAPTER SIX

THE PATH OF PROGRESS:
PRESENTING OURSELVES TO GOD

In dealing with this subject of consecration we note the increased stress on the matter of choice and action. God has done so much, but this does not permit passivity on our part. Once we have recognized what He has done for us in Christ, we are called upon to make the proper response from our side. In the fourth chapter we were commanded to "reckon"; now we are told that we must act. We could not do so before. It was futile to attempt to consecrate our old man to God, for he was unsuitable and unacceptable. As Nee reminds us: "resurrection alone has made consecration possible" (p. 101).

The Christian is a servant, but he is not servile; he obeys "from the heart." He is living in the good of resurrection life, so his whole being, including every member and faculty, is to be made available to God, held at His disposal and subject to His every wish.

This, says Nee, is the most satisfying and secure

of lives. It is logical and right, for God has literally bought us for Himself at great cost and never means to pass us over to another owner. Once we recognize this, we embark on a rewarding life of constantly referring everything back to our rightful Master, learning to like what He likes and to avoid what He dislikes.

PRESENTING OURSELVES TO GOD

BIBLE READING: Romans 6:12-23

CHAPTER SUB-HEADINGS

QUESTIONS ON CHAPTER SIX

21

CHAPTER SEVEN

THE ETERNAL PURPOSE

This remarkable chapter is so clear that it hardly permits any amplification or explanation. It constitutes not so much an interlude in the development of Nee's subjects as a background to all the rest. It takes us into God's confidence, so explaining the normal Christian life from His viewpoint. We might have passed it over all too lightly if it had been the first chapter; but since we now consider it in the light of all that we have been studying, it gives meaning and purpose to all the rest.

If we can grasp Watchman Nee's exposition of the radical difference between man as he is and man as God meant him to be, we will agree that the Cross was absolutely necessary, for the old man could have no part in this eternal purpose of God but needs to be put away and replaced by His New Man.

We must be profoundly moved by the unveiling of God's heart which shows Him to be not only Creator but a Father who longs for a family of sons and daughters. This lifts our thinking out of the academic considerations of the theologians and even the human problems of man's sin and holiness, disclosing to us what God must have suffered in His relationships with the human race. Happily it reveals also the glory of the Cross.

THE ETERNAL PURPOSE

BIBLE READING: Romans 8:16-30

CHAPTER SUB-HEADINGS

QUESTIONS ON CHAPTER SEVEN

1. What is God's unchanging purpose for man? p. 109
2. What is God's purpose for His Son in relation to man? p. 110
3. "He cannot do without me." Is this true? If so, give some reasons why God needs us. p. 111
4. What difference does Nee make between "the only begotten Son" and "the first begotten"? p. 111
5. "Abba, Father." Find the only occasion on which it is recorded that Jesus so addressed the Father, and suggest how this term accords with what has previously been said about the believer's choice of the will of God. p. 113

CHAPTER EIGHT

THE HOLY SPIRIT

This chapter is described as a digression from the main subject, but it merits special attention and is very timely. How often have the activities and gifts of the Holy Spirit become the subject of controversy and even acrimony! In our group study let us determine that we will not be betrayed into acrimony, even though we may disagree. No man has the last word on the subject, for we are dealing with the Spirit who has such infinite variety in His Person and ways that we cannot expect to confine Him or His activities to any rigid system of man's teaching.

The Spirit gives diverse experiences to different people. Nee illustrates this diversity from the Scriptures and from the history of various notable men of God. He avoids recounting his own experiences out of modest restraint, and certainly not because he lacked the enduement with power.

Most of Nee's message is devoted to an inspired setting forth of the wonder and privilege of being indwelt by the Spirit of God. It is salutary for us to appreciate that the essence of the normal Christian life is not doctrine, procedure or experience, but a Person. Nee began the book by stating that only Christ Himself has ever lived this kind of life, and now we are reminded that He has come to live it in us by the power of His Spirit.

THE HOLY SPIRIT

BIBLE READINGS: Acts 2:32-39; Romans 8:1-17

CHAPTER SUB-HEADINGS

QUESTIONS ON CHAPTER EIGHT

1. What are the two aspects of the gift of Spirit? Which is the most precious, and why?   p. 123
2. What is God's purpose in pouring out His Spirit on men?   p. 126
3. "Is it possible that *He* has been glorified and *you* have not received the Spirit?" Does this relate to the enduement with power or the indwelling, or both?   p. 127
4. Is the experience of the young Christian man a contradiction of Christ's words in Luke 11:13?   p. 129
5. What three things are mentioned together with the Holy Spirit in Acts 2:38-39?   p. 131
6. Which is more likely: that the one con-

THE MEANING AND VALUE
OF ROMANS SEVEN

As Nee remarks on Romans 7, the chapter itself seems negative and impractical, and yet it corresponds so accurately to the common experience of many Christians that it must be more important than might have been thought.

We may have imagined that bondage to the law was not really our problem. We have appreciated that for Paul and his Jewish contemporaries the Law represented the complete opposite of the Gospel. We noted in Galatians how the truth and power of the Gospel can be nullified by a reversion to "works of the law," but may have imagined that this all related to Jewish practices and was therefore of little importance to us today.

We now find that this is far from being so, for Nee tells us that this is a major consideration in the spiritual growth of all believers, and that "the Law" is a much bigger issue than we had realized, being the inclusive term for all the requirements and standards of divine holiness. It is, in fact, the will of God. After reaching my present state of spiritual experience, I *want* to do God's will. Of course I do. Then why do I so often fail? Paul makes no secret of the fact that this was his problem before he discovered the remedy, and he implies that something of this kind must happen to every man before he can enjoy the fullness described in Romans 8.

THE MEANING AND VALUE OF ROMANS SEVEN

BIBLE READING: Romans 7:1-25

CHAPTER SUB-HEADINGS

QUESTIONS ON CHAPTER NINE

1. Do you think that the section of Romans 7 from verse 7 to 25 could ever have described the experience of Saul before his conversion? Or of any other unconverted man?   p. 152
2. Find the number of times in which "I," "me," or "my" appear in this section (7-25). Can you indicate what this suggests?   p. 153
3. Describe the difference between "law" and "grace."   p. 155
4. "We need to have our weakness proved to ourselves beyond dispute." Does this kind of proof come to a lax or self-centered Christian?   p. 158
5. Did God ever expect men to fulfill His Law?   p. 159
6. Does the Law of the Lord Jesus demand

33

less of us than the Law of Moses? p. 161

7. "If the Law will never pass away, then how can I ever be united to Christ?" Answer this in your own words. p. 161

8. What does Nee say about the value of coming to despair of ever pleasing God? p. 165

9. This story of the drowning man is excellent to illustrate the need for ceasing from self-effort, but does it suggest a false analogy as to what it means to be saved? p. 168

10. The man who cried "Who will deliver me...?" afterwards gives thanks but does not say how or when he was delivered. Can you suggest why this is so? p. 171

CHAPTER TEN

THE PATH OF PROGRESS: WALKING IN THE SPIRIT

Nee defines living "in Adam" as knowing "in experience all Adam's very complete provision for sinning," and remarks that we have all found this most effective in its outworking. He now proposes to deal with that feature of being "in Christ" which is its absolute antithesis, namely, enjoying in experience the complete provision by the Spirit for righteous living.

Some may find this chapter less stimulating, not because they disagree with what is stated but because Nee seems to give but little instruction. It is, however, very difficult to tell people how to walk. You can demonstrate walking to them; you can give some support to them as they make a move; and you can encourage them to take further steps. This is rather what Nee tries to do. There is no formula for walking other than to choose your direction, to summon up the strength given to you, and then use it.

So the Christian's life becomes a succession of miracles—the lame man walks!

WALKING IN THE SPIRIT

BIBLE READINGS: Romans 8:1-17;
                Galatians 5:13-25

CHAPTER SUB-HEADINGS

QUESTIONS ON CHAPTER TEN

CHAPTER ELEVEN

ONE BODY IN CHRIST

Nee now leaps over the parenthetical chapters concerning Israel and passes directly from Romans 8 to Romans 12, with its insistence that the normal Christian life is corporate in its character: "We who are many are one body" (Romans 12:5).

Those who find it difficult to follow the details of Nee's allegorical allusions to Adam and his partner, Eve, should remember that while we must not base doctrines on allegories or parables, we can often get fresh light on truth by means of them. The point which Nee seeks to derive from the story is that the Church, composed of Jews and Gentiles, is no by-product of God's dealings with men, no after-thought in the redemptive work of the Cross, but God's original intention for the human race.

This chapter brings us to yet another contrast between life in Christ and life in Adam. The latter is essentially individualistic, whereas the normal Christian life is just the opposite. By His Cross Christ not only made me one with Himself; He made me also one with my fellow believers. It is my old man who demands independence; the New Man is a harmonious Body of many interdependent members whose unity is maintained by the Cross which sets aside personal ideas and wishes in favor of the will of God.

ONE BODY IN CHRIST

BIBLE READINGS: Romans 12:1-5;
Ephesians 5:22-33

CHAPTER SUB-HEADINGS

QUESTIONS ON CHAPTER ELEVEN

CHAPTER TWELVE

THE CROSS AND THE SOUL LIFE

It is not generally appreciated that while the Holy Spirit desires to govern and use both our bodies and our souls, He does not make His headquarters in our soul but lives in our spirit (small letter "s"). In Adam's case, on the day when he sinned his spirit died—as God had said it would—which means that he lost all inner communication with God. Now in Christ believers have been made alive, that is, they have vital communication with God in the realm of the renewed spirit (Romans 8:16).

By the Cross God has provided for the imbalance caused by the Fall, delivering the Christian from having a life governed by the power of his own soul. We readily understand that man must not be governed by his body, for that reduces him to the level of the beasts, but we do not so readily appreciate that he must not be governed by his soul either, for that leaves him a creature of independence, obliged to hold his own ideas and make his own decisions without dependence on God.

Salvation should consist in having our souls restored, i.e., removed from their usurped position of authority in our lives and subordinated to our spirit's cooperation with the Holy Spirit.

THE CROSS AND THE SOUL LIFE

BIBLE READINGS: Luke 14:25-27;
                  2 Corinthians 5:14-18

CHAPTER SUB-HEADINGS

QUESTIONS ON CHAPTER TWELVE

1. How does Nee describe the action of
   "bearing the cross"?   P. 223
2. "Adam was created neutral." Is this still
   true of:
       (a) Unregenerate men?
       (b) Christian men?   p. 225
3. Name some of the possible ways by
   which the life of the Son of God can be
   confined and crowded almost out of
   action in our service for God.   p. 228
4. Find some statements in John's Gospel
   in which Jesus said that He could not act
   on His own. Was He confessing literal
   incapacity or referring to the exercise of
   His choice in the matter?   p. 230
5. What proofs does Nee give to identify
   that which springs from the natural life? p. 232

CHAPTER THIRTEEN

THE PATH OF PROGRESS: BEARING THE CROSS

In this chapter Nee reminds us that the principle of death and resurrection power was proved and taught by the Lord Jesus, even before He died on the Cross. His own service was preceded by the symbolic acceptance of death which was portrayed by His baptism in the waters of Jordan; and His repeated appeal to His disciples to take up their own Cross was His declaration that only by this means can a man serve God as he should.

Unlike the once-for-all aspect, taught earlier, of the putting away of the old man by crucifixion, this aspect of the Cross's work is shown now to be one calling for constant renewal: the Cross must be taken up daily. Nee has a very helpful comment: "The Cross has borne me: now I must bear it."

BEARING THE CROSS

BIBLE READINGS: Matthew 10:34-39; Mark 8:32-35; Luke 17:32-34; John 12:24-26

CHAPTER SUB-HEADINGS

QUESTIONS ON CHAPTER THIRTEEN

8. "Do you like the will of God?" To be a

CHAPTER FOURTEEN

THE GOAL OF THE GOSPEL

I find it impossible to comment on this chapter without remarking that Watchman Nee seems almost to be foretelling his own future. It is clear that he was already able to apply this message on *Waste* to his own history, but neither he who spoke so movingly nor we who listened with great profit had any idea of the future which lay before him.

For twenty years he was "poured out" in suffering for Christ's sake. Men misjudged, as they did in the case of Mary, but surely there was a fragrance to God from Nee's prison cell. He need not have been in Red China. It was out of a sense of loyalty to his many brothers and sisters in Christ that, when he could easily have moved away from the Communist territory to fresh fields of service, he decided rather to stay and suffer with them. Outside of China there was a great open door; so many areas to be evangelized, so many Christians to be instructed, that even many of Nee's friends felt it a waste for him to submit to the inevitable betrayal and the bitter sufferings which awaited him. Here he tells us that Christ intended the preaching of the Gospel to issue in the kind of costly self-sacrifice made by Mary. To God's glory we acknowledge that it did so issue in the life of Watchman Nee.

A preacher discovers that he is tested by his own words. Let him publicly affirm that any given course is the will of God and he will be privately put to the proof as to whether it is true in his own case. The same thing may happen for those who study this book. If, after consideration of the final chapter, you decide that God's greatest pleasure is served by those who are ready to "waste" themselves on Him, then you can be sure that in your own circumstances, sooner or later, and probably sooner, you yourself will be faced with the challenge.

"The principle of waste is the principle of power." We have no means of knowing the practical results in China of the breaking of Watchman Nee's own alabaster box. We do know that the messages contained in this book we have been studying have carried the fragrance of Christ into most countries of the world. They continue to do so even after the speaker, having died in the Lord, rests now from his labors.

Dare we honestly face Nee's final challenge? "When we see Him face to face, I trust that we shall all break and pour out everything for Him. But *today*—what are we doing *today*?"

THE GOAL OF THE GOSPEL

BIBLE READINGS: Matthew 26:6-13; Mark 14:3-9; John 12:1-8

CHAPTER SUB-HEADINGS

QUESTIONS ON CHAPTER FOURTEEN

use of the word "beforehand"?   p. 278

8. Can you suggest modern parallels to this act of breaking the flask of alabaster for the Lord?   p. 281

9. Mary's gift was gladly received. The rich young ruler's was regretfully declined (Mark 10:21). What was the difference?

10. Find in 2 Corinthians 2 a reference to Christians being "a sweet savour of Christ."   p. 281

This book was produced by the Christian Literature Crusade. We hope it has been helpful to you in living the Christian life. CLC is a literature mission with ministry in over 50 countries worldwide. If you would like to know more about us, or are interested in opportunities to serve with a faith mission, we invite you to write to:

Christian Literature Crusade
P.O. Box 1449
Fort Washington, PA 19034